Ga Ting

家
庭

Ga Ting
家
庭

Minh Ly

Ga Ting
家庭
first published 2017 by
Scirocco Drama
An imprint of J. Gordon Shillingford Publishing Inc.

Scirocco Drama Editor: Glenda MacFarlane
Cover design by Terry Gallagher / Doowah Design Inc.
Author photo by Denise Grant
Production photos by Raymund Shum
Printed and bound in Canada on 100% post-consumer recycled paper.

We acknowledge the financial support of the Manitoba Arts Council and The Canada Council for the Arts for our publishing program.

Production inquiries should be addressed to:
info@minhly.ca

Library and Archives Canada Cataloguing in Publication

Ly, Minh, author
Ga ting / Minh Ly. -- 1st edition.

Includes some text in Cantonese.
ISBN 978-1-927922-29-3 (softcover)

I. Title.

PS8623.Y23G3 2017 C812'.6 C2017-900958-3

J. Gordon Shillingford Publishing
P.O. Box 86, RPO Corydon Avenue, Winnipeg, MB Canada R3M 3S3

To my

GA TING (family)

家
庭

in life, work and art.

Minh Ly

Minh Ly is a Canadian actor/writer based out of Toronto. He trained at Studio 58, an acting conservatory in Vancouver. Since graduating from his alma mater, Minh has worked extensively in film, TV, and theatre. Minh's playwriting experience includes having performed his solo show, *White, Another F# $king Identity Piece!* at BC Buds, a new works festival at the Firehall Theatre in Vancouver.

Ga Ting is his first professionally produced full-length play. It premiered in 2014, co-produced by the frank theatre and VACT in Richmond, BC. In 2016 it was remounted by the frank theatre, and presented by The Cultch in Vancouver; both productions garnered sold-out houses.

Minh is an ardent proponent for inclusivity in our industry. He hopes that with more artists in marginalized communities having the opportunity to tell stories that can connect with a broader audience, our Canadian theatre community will better reflect the society we all live in.

www.minhly.ca

Acknowledgements

I would like to give a special thanks to Chris Gatchalian at the frank theatre and Donna Yamamoto at Vancouver Asian Canadian Theatre for seeing something in my play that led to two impactful productions, and now a published book.

Ga Ting wouldn't be in its current form without the artists who were involved in the workshops and productions; from the bottom of my heart, I thank you all.

Finally, I would like to acknowledge my parents' unwavering love and support. They came to this country with nothing, but gave me everything. They are my heartbeat...

Ly Nguu Tu and Ly Thi Mai, I thank you...and I love you.

Foreword

As the show's producer, I have sometimes described *Ga Ting* as "*Guess Who's Coming to Dinner* with a dark, queer Asian twist." This reductive précis may work for promotional purposes, but it fails to do justice to the play's nuanced, generous humanity.

The story of *Ga Ting* is simple. Matthew, a young Caucasian accountant from Vancouver, flies to Toronto to meet Hong and Mai, the parents of his Chinese ex-boyfriend Kevin, who has recently died. The discussion that ensues over dinner reveals not only the order of events that led to Kevin's death, but the intercultural and intergenerational tensions at the heart of contemporary Canadian society.

When the frank theatre company decided to produce the play's world premiere in 2014, we knew we had a play the likes of which Vancouver—and perhaps even Canada—had never truly seen before. While the play's "coming out" aspect may have been familiar, its specific cultural context and especially its bilingualism—the play, as you will see, is performed in both English and Mandarin—was not. While strides have certainly been made during the last two decades vis-à-vis culturally diversifying our stages, Canadian theatre, on the whole, remains sharply disconnected from the country's current and ever-evolving demographic realities.

the frank theatre and our co-producers, Vancouver Asian Canadian Theatre, decided to present the play at the Richmond Cultural Centre in Richmond, a politically conservative, heavily Chinese suburb of Vancouver. I was both excited and nervous about the choice. Excited because it was evidence of our thinking outside the box and creating an opportunity to reach out to new, diverse audiences; nervous because of my own assumptions about how an ostensibly socially conservative community might respond to the play's subject matter.

The show played to capacity houses over its two-week run. The audience for the show was the most diverse I had seen in my entire life, vis-à-vis race, age, ability and sexual orientation. Audience members of Chinese descent talked not only about how it was the first time they had gone to live theatre and heard their language included as an integral, dynamic, non-negotiable part of the play; more fundamentally, they said it was the first time they had seen *a reflection of themselves*. If you believe, as I do, that one of the primary duties of theatre is to offer concrete, embodied validation of an audience's experiences and existence, then *Ga Ting* did this for audience members who had never before experienced such validation from a play. In this sense, *Ga Ting* is a revolutionary piece of theatre.

I must add that if novelty is all this play has going for it, it would not have affected and impacted as many people as it has. The play's strength is its refusal to succumb to dualism. There are no good guys or bad guys—the traditional Chinese parents may be uninformed about queerness, but they are well-meaning, hard-working folks who genuinely loved their child. The Caucasian lover, as expected, holds mainstream liberal Canadian values, but, like most white Canadians, is co-opted by structural racism in ways he himself is not fully aware.

Ga Ting's success can be attributed in part to the precise time in which it premiered—near the end of the right-wing Harper era, when there was pushback against the past decade's cultural homogenization and a yen to confront and celebrate difference. But because it is, at its core, a compassionate, yet honest, representation of the human experiment that is Canada, it is a play that, I believe, will be produced for many years to come.

C. E. Gatchalian
Playwright & Artistic Producer of the frank theatre company
January 2017

Production History

Ga Ting premiered at the Richmond Cultural Centre in Richmond BC on March 22nd 2014, co-produced by the frank theatre and Vancouver Asian Canadian Theatre, with the following cast and creative team:

Hong Lee.................................... BC Lee
Mai Lee............................ Alannah Ong
Matthew .... Michael Antonakos

Directed by Rick Tae
Set and Costume Design by Christopher David Gauthier
Lighting Design by Gerald King
Sound Design by Heath Whitelock
Projections Design: Ian Chan
Stage Management: Shannon Macelli

Ga Ting had a second mounting presented by The Cultch in Vancouver BC, produced by the frank theatre, which opened on March 8th 2016 with the following cast and creative team:

Hong Lee.................................... BC Lee

Mai Lee............................. Alannah Ong

Matthew........................... Brian J Sutton

Directed by Rick Tae

Set and Costume Design by Christopher David Gauthier

Lighting Design by Gerald King

Sound Design by Heath Whitelock

Projections Design: Ian Chan

Stage Management: Shannon Macelli

Ga Ting also had support from the Canada Council for the Arts.

The 2016 cast of *Ga Ting*: BC Lee as Hong Lee, Alannah Ong as Mai Lee and Brian J Sutton as Matthew.

Hong consoling Mai (BC Lee and Alannah Ong).

Hong takes control of the situation
(Alannah Ong, BC Lee, and Brian J Sutton).

Hong having a final moment with his son (BC Lee).

Playwright's Notes

The seed which grew and developed into *Ga Ting* began as an idea, one that had been planted years before it came to fruition onstage. It started with an image I had in mind: an image of a middle aged Asian couple-sitting, talking, eating, and connecting with a young Caucasian man. But why would these seemingly polarized people be together? What would they have to talk about? By driving their conversation forward through places we fear to go, *Ga Ting* became my answer to those questions.

I have seen and read a variety of queer-themed theatre written by fellow Canadian playwrights whom I admire. However, I have yet to encounter a piece that explores the cultural implications of homosexuality that I grew up with; specifically, the fact that homosexuality is taboo in some Chinese and other ethnic communities. *Ga Ting* aims to bring those issues to the forefront in our theatres.

The story is told through a distinctly Chinese-Canadian lens, focusing on a cultural and generational divide. But at its core, this is a play about breaking down the walls we construct between ourselves and the ones we love; in particular, the walls between parents and their children. Whether it leads to a simple gesture, an act of understanding, a hug, or perhaps a look of acceptance, my hope is that this play will bring families closer together.

Characters

Hong Lee .... The father, Chinese, late 50s

Mai Lee .... The mother, Chinese, 50s

Matthew................... The boyfriend, Caucasian, late 20s / early 30s

Production Notes

Bold text represents dialogue spoken in CHINESE.

Surtitles are projected to translate ENGLISH into CHINESE, and CHINESE into ENGLISH.

"Flashbacks" are initiated with an ocean wave sound effect; these scenes from the past begin at the "fall of the ocean wave." An ocean wave also brings the play back to the "Present." Perhaps projections can help support the setting of the flashbacks.

Act I

Lights up to reveal MAI and HONG's home. A living room leads into an open kitchen with a dining table. The floors are hardwood. Chinese calligraphy adorns the walls, as do a couple of Chinese paintings (anything but a bamboo painting). The space is very full of items collected throughout the years. Perhaps a Chinese shrine cabinet is in the living room, with a couple of Chinese god statues.

MATTHEW is wandering around the living area, shamelessly touching and looking at items. MAI is in the kitchen finishing up cooking dinner, and she is wearing an apron. There is definitely a rice cooker in the kitchen.

MATTHEW arrived from the airport a few minutes earlier. He is dressed well, with a fitted T-shirt, perhaps, and a blazer. His carry-on is in the living room, and so is a wrapped canvas. There is a vase with bamboo in it on the coffee table. After nosing around for a few minutes, MATTHEW picks up a picture frame with a younger MAI and HONG at a beach in Vietnam when MAI approaches.

MAI: That was long time ago. We very young.

MATTHEW: I can see that, you looked good! I mean, you still look good now, for your age…

MAI: Is okay, I know I'm old. Sit, dinner almost ready.

MATTHEW: You really didn't have to go to all the trouble. I could have ordered something in, or taken you both out. Do you like steak? There's always The Keg.

MAI: Oh no. Don't be silly. We prefer eat in. This is no trouble. You go to trouble. *(Gesturing to the bamboo.)* No need bring present.

MATTHEW: The bamboo? It's nothing. Thought you would like it…and by the looks of things, I think it fits right in.

MAI: I like, thank you.

MATTHEW: So…dinner's almost ready?

MAI: Ah yes! *(MAI continues to put dinner together.)* I cook much better before. Now not so good, cook not so much. Only two people live here, easy to get food at restaurant before we come home. We eat very little now. When you get old, you worry about everything. Too much cholesterol, too much fat, too much…uh, sodium, too much sugar, eat too much. So we eat not so much. So, I cook very little.

MATTHEW: I'm sure everything will be delicious. It smells great.

MAI: Hope you like. Better than The Keg.

MATTHEW: Does Mr. Lee need any help?

MAI: No, he is okay.

MATTHEW: You sure? I'm not much of a handyman but I can try to help. Kevin usually fixed things around the house.

MAI: Yes?

MATTHEW: Well, more like, design things and choose the wall colours.

MAI: Yes, he always very creative. Since Kevin young boy he love drawing. Start with crayons. Ah... anyway, Mr. Lee is fine. All day he have time to fix washroom sink. But no, he have to wait for you to come before fixing sink. He will come down soon. Relax, Matthew, sit down.

MATTHEW: Okay.

MATTHEW sits.

MAI: Oh no!

MATTHEW: What's wrong?

MAI: I give you nothing to drink.

MATTHEW: I'm fine. Don't worry about me.

MAI: We have apple juice...water...and milk—we have milk. I say to Mr. Lee, buy some beer, but he forget.

MATTHEW: Really Mrs. Lee, I'm fine. I prefer wine anyways. I'm really into Malbecs lately.

MAI: Mao-bec.

MATTHEW: It's a purple grape variety—a type of red wine.

MAI: I'm sorry, I have no Mao-bec.

MATTHEW: That's okay, I was just saying, I didn't mean I wanted any.

MAI: Mr. Lee does this all the time. Wait and wait last minute, then forget what I ask him to do.

MATTHEW: You know what? I would love a glass of water.

MAI: Water?

MATTHEW: Yes.

MAI: I get you water.

MAI gets MATTHEW a glass of water; she pours it from a Brita filter container.

MAI: Your flight was good?

MATTHEW: Yes.

MAI: I tell you call us when you get to Toronto airport, Mr. Lee can go get you. Raining all day. But you did not call…

MATTHEW: It stopped raining, and I just ended up calling an Uber. It was fine.

MAI: Uber?

MATTHEW: It's an app on your phone, you put in your location and—

MAI: I know Uber. I use all the time when Mr. Lee is too busy to drive me. I have very good smart phone, touch screen. Like magic.

MATTHEW: Haha…I know, it's crazy what things phones can do these days.

MAI: I worry, Matthew. I think you get lost.

MATTHEW: Just a delayed flight.

MAI: It's okay, you here now…plane delay all the time. Good weather, bad weather. All the same. They always delay.

MATTHEW: Sorry about that.

MAI: Not your fault. You not fly the plane. Food not ready, so I am the one who is sorry.

MATTHEW: It's no big deal Mrs. Lee, I'm not even hungry yet.

MAI: Call me Mai.

MATTHEW: Okay…well, you can call me Matt.

MAI: Matt.

MATTHEW: Yes.

MAI: Matt.

MATTHEW: Yes, that's it.

MAI: Matt.

MATTHEW: Yup, that's my name.

MAI: I like that name. Matt. Good name. Matt mean something?

MATTHEW: Yes, I googled it once…it actually came from the Hebrew name Matityahu, and means "Gift from God." No surprise there, right? *(Short beat.)* Just kidding. The Greek version of Matthew is Mattathias, which means "divine."

Beat.

MAI: Very nice. I don't know what "Kevin" mean, but his Chinese name mean Ocean. More simple. It's—

MATTHEW: "Hoi."

MAI: Yes! Yes! Hoi. He tell you?

MATTHEW: Yeah, he told me. My name isn't quite as… beautifully simple.

MAI: No. I like.

MATTHEW: Thank you.

HONG enters. MATTHEW leaps to his feet to be polite.

HONG: **The food is not ready yet?**
還沒有飯吃呀?

MAI: **Almost.**
差不多啦.

HONG: **I'm starving.**
餓啦.

MAI: **Wait a little.**
快啦.

HONG looks at MATTHEW. MATTHEW looks at HONG. Beat.

MATTHEW: Hi, I'm Matthew…or Matt for short.

HONG leans in to shake MATTHEW's hand.

HONG: Yes. Hong…Hong for short.

MATTHEW: Haha…yeah, that's funny…

HONG: Yes, I am funny man. All the time my friends say to me, "Hong, you so funny!"

Beat. HONG gets himself something to drink.

MATTHEW: Faucets all fixed…(*about to say 'Hong' but thinks better of it*)…Mr. Lee?

HONG: Yes.

MAI: Matt bring us present.

MATTHEW: It's nothing, really.

MATTHEW offers the bamboo to HONG.

MAI: Bamboo.

HONG: Mm. Very…original.

MATTHEW: I thought you would like it.

HONG: Yes, of course.

MATTHEW: How's your weekend been?

HONG: Good.

Beat.

MATTHEW: Excuse me, can I use your washroom for a sec?

MAI: Yes, yes, door there, turn right.

MATTHEW: Thanks, wash my hands before dinner. Germs on a flight you know?

MATTHEW exits.

MAI: **Why are you being so weird?**
你古里古怪的做什麼?

HONG: **I am trying to make conversation.**
我在找話說.

MAI: **Don't be mean.**
別那麼尖酸.

HONG: **I don't know what you're talking about.**
不知道你在說什麼.

MAI: **Please be nice to him.**
對人家客氣點.

HONG: **Okay, okay…hurry up, I'm hungry.**
得了得了, 快點開飯吧, 我餓死了.

MAI: **I'm serious.**
我可是認真的.

HONG: **I know.**
知道了.

MAI: **Help me get the rice.**
去盛飯!

HONG grabs some bowls of rice and brings them to the dinner table. MATTHEW enters.

MAI: Almost ready, Matt.

MATTHEW: Can I help?

MAI: No. You sit.

MATTHEW: Okay.

MATTHEW sits. MAI and HONG finish getting the table ready. MAI lights candles.

You have a nice home.

MAI: Thank you. When you get old, all you have is home. So have to take care.

MATTHEW: It shows. Love the hardwood.

HONG: Hm.

MAI: One more candle.

HONG: Candles. She love candles.

MAI: Good after cooking. Get rid of frying smell.

MATTHEW: I like the smell of a kitchen after some cooking.

HONG: Candle just cover it up.

MATTHEW: Well…I like candles too. Ginger peach?

MAI: Ginger peach?

MATTHEW: That candle, the scent, it smells like ginger peach.

MAI: I don't know…*(MAI picks up the candle, and reads the label on the bottom of it.)* Yes, yes, "ginger peach." Wah, you have very good nose.

MATTHEW: I used to work part-time at a home décor store when I was in school. We had candles aplenty.

MAI: Candles of plenty?

MATTHEW: Plenty of candles…lots…

MAI: A lot—

MATTHEW: Yes…scented candles…lots…of candles.

HONG and MAI stare at him, blank-faced.

MATTHEW: I like the smell of a well-used kitchen and candles…together, it's great.

MAI is now seated as well.

MAI: Yes…great, very great. Enough candle talk. Start eating…eat!

HONG is already eating. Beat.

MAI: You need fork?

MATTHEW: I can use chopsticks just fine.

MAI: Eat!

MATTHEW hesitates.

MAI: Something wrong? You not like the food?

MATTHEW: No, it's just…I imagined this moment. Meeting you both over dinner, and believe it or not, this is kind of how I pictured it. This setting, the plates…everything. It just feels surreal that this is finally happening. I was taking it all in. Everything looks fantastic.

MAI: Thank you. Eat a lot. I don't want left-over.

MATTHEW delves into the food. Beat.

MAI: We cannot wait for you to come. Right, Hong?

HONG: Hmhmm. I could not sleep last night. So excited.

MAI: **What are you saying?**
你在講什麼?

HONG: **I said I couldn't sleep last night, because I was so excited.**
我一夜難眠就是為了太興奮啦.

MAI slaps HONG on the shoulder.

MAI: Anyway…we meet at last.

MATTHEW: Yes…at last.

Beat. HONG is scarfing down a lot of food.

MAI: **Don't eat so fast.**
做什麼吃這麼快?

HONG: **I told you I'm hungry**
我說過我餓啦.

Beat.

MATTHEW: You made a lot of food.

HONG: Because you are here.

MAI: **It's because he's here that there's so much food. You should be happy.**
你是託他的福才有那麼多好菜吃. 你才該高興.

HONG: **I am happy, very happy.**
高興, 我當然高興.

MATTHEW: Did I say something?

MAI: What you mean?

MATTHEW: Is something wrong?

MAI: No, no. Nothing wrong. *(MAI eyes HONG.)*

HONG: Nothing wrong.

MAI: **Thank him for the gift.**
謝謝人家的禮物呀.

HONG: **What gift?**
什麼禮物?

MAI: **The bamboo!**
竹子呀.

HONG: **I thanked him already.**
不是謝過了嗎?

MAI: **No, you didn't .**
沒有.

MATTHEW: Woah, there's a lot of talking going on!

HONG: Ah…thank you for bamboo.

MATTHEW: You're welcome. I was told bamboo brings good fortune.

HONG: Hmhmm.

Beat. Everyone eats.

MATTHEW: How long have you lived in Toronto?

MAI: Long time…we move here from Vietnam and stay here.

MATTHEW: You might have loved Vancouver. You get the ocean, mountains and a ton of beaches.

HONG: Beaches in Toronto too.

MATTHEW: I'm sure there is, I was just—

MAI: Yes, when Kevin a little kid, we take him all the time to…Wasaga Beach. It was his favourite… so much energy, always run around the sand. But one time…

Flashback to when KEVIN was a child. MAI and HONG are watching KEVIN at the beach.

HONG: **Mai, where is Kevin?**

阿美，凱文呢?

MAI: **He is just over there, in the water with the other kids.**

他跟其他小朋友在那邊玩水.

HONG: **You let him go by himself?**

你就讓他一個人去玩?

MAI: **He's fine.**

沒問題的啦.

HONG: **Mai, I think something's wrong, he's not moving.**

有點不妥. 他沒在動.

MAI: **What? Let's go down there. Kevin! Kevin!**

什麼, 下去看看, 凱文! 凱文!

HONG: **Oh, wait…he's moving again, he's fine. Scared me to death.**

等一等, 他在動了, 沒事, 嚇死我了.

MAI: **That's not funny, Kevin. Don't you ever scare your father and me like that again.**

凱文, 這不能開玩笑, 以後不可以這樣嚇我和你爸.

HONG: **Did you teach him how to float in the water?**
是你教他浮水的?

MAI: **No, I can't even float.**
沒有, 我自己都不會.

HONG: **Kevin, you're still laughing? Stop laughing this instant. Never do that again, it scared us to death. Stop it!**
凱文, 你還笑. 不准笑. 以後不可以這樣, 把我們都嚇到了.還笑!

Present.

MAI: To this day, we still don't know who teach him to float.

MATTHEW: Maybe he taught himself when you weren't looking.

HONG: I always looking.

MATTHEW: Really? Always? That's impossible.

HONG: Possible.

MATTHEW: You can't always have your eyes on someone.

HONG: Possible.

MATTHEW: Impossible.

HONG: Possible.

MATTHEW: Okay, how many pieces of bok choy has Mai eaten so far?

HONG: Stupid question, I not looking.

MATTHEW: See?

HONG: I watch Kevin closely before, he was baby and my son. Mai my wife. After we marry, no need to watch so closely. She is grown-up woman. Will not choke on bok choy.

MATTHEW: I don't know what we're talking about anymore.

MAI: We talking about how Kevin surprise us all the time. He do things when we not looking.

HONG: I always looking.

MAI: **Enough**. (夠了.) Kevin always know what he want.

MATTHEW: Yes, he did.

Beat. More eating.

How are you two doing…with everything? I mean…

HONG: Good. Fine.

MATTHEW: You sure?

HONG: You expect another answer?

MATTHEW: No. It's just…it can't be—

MAI: We are his parents. We do our best. It is hard… but we try. How are you…with everything?

MATTHEW: It hasn't been easy, but of course we all…have to move on eventually.

Beat.

I'm sorry…I didn't mean it that way.

MAI: It is okay.

Beat.

MATTHEW: How was the funeral? Everything went smoothly?

MAI: Yes.

MATTHEW: So...I can't help but wonder why I wasn't invited?

HONG: The food is very good today.

MATTHEW: Why wasn't I invited to the funeral?

HONG: We forget.

MATTHEW: Tell me why?

HONG: You are not family.

MATTHEW: But I am—I mean...I was.

HONG: No.

MAI: What Mr. Lee mean is—

MATTHEW: I was very much a part of Kevin's family. So were his friends.

HONG: Not blood.

MATTHEW: Just because I'm not blood, doesn't mean I didn't love him. I called and called...left messages...sent you a letter about Kevin I wanted to share at the funeral. I tried to find out what was going on, but no one got back to me.

MAI: Too soon, we did not know what to do with... you and Kevin and...

MATTHEW: Kevin's funeral was my chance to say goodbye to him. I just wish you could've given me that.

HONG: What you want now? Us to say we sorry? It happen.

MATTHEW: I want to understand why you couldn't have included me.

HONG: You have no idea what we go through. You only think what you want. What you think is right. You give money for funeral? You organize everything? You raise Kevin from baby to big man? You know him two, three years. That is all. *(To MAI.)* **The soup is also very good tonight.** (今晚的湯很好.)

MATTHEW: What did you just say?

HONG: I said the soup is very good tonight. Have some and shut up.

MAI: **Hong!**

阿鴻!

MATTHEW: I should have been at the funeral.

HONG: You come to mine! And it happen very soon if you keep talking like this.

MAI: **Choy, choy, choy…don't say things like that!** (睬!睬!睬! 講這什麼呀. 阿修, 我了解你的傷痛.) I understand why you upset, Matt.

HONG: **We owe him nothing. He didn't need to be there.**

我們可沒欠他的. 沒必要讓他在那場合出現.

MAI: **We should have invited him.** (我們應給讓他來的.) *(Beat.)* Matthew, when Kevin died, it was all too much, we cannot handle. Too much family visit already. But tomorrow…if you want, we can take you to cemetery.

Beat.

MATTHEW: I would like that.

HONG: **I don't have time.**
我沒空.

MAI: **Then I will go by myself.**
那我自己去.

HONG: **It's too far to bus.**
坐巴士太遠.

MAI: **Then I will ask my sister to drive us.**
我叫我姊帶我們去.

MATTHEW: All I'm saying is what happened, how you dealt with everything, I don't think Kevin would have wanted it like that.

MAI: I know…

MATTHEW: I want you to understand…that it—

MAI: We understand. I am sorry that you not there.

MATTHEW: Thank you, Mai.

HONG: You get apology. Happy now?

MATTHEW: We'll visit the cemetery tomorrow then?

MAI: Yes…**Hong**? (好的, 阿鴻?)

HONG: **It's your problem, do whatever you want.**
你的事, 跟我無關.

HONG gets up and serves himself some more rice from the rice cooker.

MATTHEW: I understand that this is hard for you, Mr. Lee. It's just…I miss him too.

Beat.

MAI: How long you stay in Toronto?

MATTHEW: A couple days, meetings with a few clients.

MAI: What do you do?

MATTHEW: For work?

MAI: Yes.

MATTHEW: I'm an accountant.

HONG: You do tax?

MATTHEW: Not exactly. I work for KPMG, a big accounting firm.

MAI: Oh.

MATTHEW: I know, you probably would have expected me to be in something more…creative, design-oriented. Something with more pizazz!

MAI: No.

MATTHEW: Truth is, I like stability. I started off as a clerk, now I'm an auditor. We got a few new accounts in Toronto, that's why I'm here. Basically my job's to analyze numbers to help maximize profits.

MAI: You enjoy?

MATTHEW: It's a job. Not everyone's lucky enough to love what they do for work.

HONG: A job should be like that. You don't need to love it.

MATTHEW: But it—

HONG: Work is just work. Do you make good money?

MAI whacks HONG.

MATTHEW: I do well enough, but I'm definitely not rich.

HONG: Good. I not open restaurant because I love it. I open restaurant because I need it. And after twenty years I still do not love it.

MATTHEW: You must love it a little…

HONG: Need. Not love.

MAI: *(To HONG.)* **Enough, enough.** (夠了,夠了.)

(To MATTHEW.) Try this, you did not have any yet.

MAI puts some food in MATTHEW's bowl.

MATTHEW: Sure…hmmm, yummy.

MAI: Yummy?

MATTHEW: I meant…tasty.

MAI: Please, tell us more…about yourself.

MATTHEW: Sure, but I really don't know what else to say.

MAI: Anything.

MATTHEW: Um…I was born and raised in Vancouver. You don't find many of those there. Trust me, everyone seems to be flying in from everywhere else.

MAI: Yes…

MATTHEW: And I got my undergrad at UBC. I eventually landed myself a corporate job…lucky me.

MAI: What else?

MATTHEW: Well…my favourite colour's blue, this is my third time in Toronto…and…I really loved your son, and have always wanted to meet his parents. I wish this happened earlier, when he was—

HONG: Why?

MATTHEW: Because you're his family.

HONG: No need.

MATTHEW: Mr. Lee, we were boyfriends. All of us should have gotten together a long time ago.

HONG: For what? To talk about what? No need before for you to come.

MATTHEW: But enough of a reason for us to meet now?

HONG: Mai think so.

MAI: If we know what we know now, we maybe meet before. But we not know you then, Matt. Kevin not say much about you. And when he pass, we so busy with funeral, family visit, no time to answer your messages. When you call again a few weeks ago, everything settle down, so…we are here. Please understand.

MATTHEW: Yes, here we are.

MAI: You meet us now.

Beat.

Kevin meet your parents?

MATTHEW: He did, a couple months in. They adored him.

HONG: Of course.

MATTHEW: What do you mean, "of course"?

HONG: You people always so open-minded. Accepting everyone, and you—

MATTHEW: —"You people"?

HONG: Caucasian, white, Greek, French, English, you all look the same…

MATTHEW: You're generalizing.

HONG: Generalizing?

MATTHEW: To talk about a large group being the—

HONG: I know what it mean.

MATTHEW: So?

HONG: So, I should not "generalize"?

MATTHEW: I wouldn't do that to you.

HONG: Oh no? What about bamboo?

MATTHEW: Do you not like it?

MAI: No, Matt, we love it.

HONG: Why bamboo? Why not lilac?

MAI: Some more soup!

MATTHEW: I just thought—

HONG: You just thought that all Asian people—do you even know what background we are?

MATTHEW: Yes, of course, you're Chinese.

HONG: We are Korean.

MATTHEW: What? Weren't you just speaking Chinese? Oh my God, I'm—

HONG: Of course we are Chinese! Do you see any kimchi on the table?

MATTHEW: No—

HONG: And we have a Chinese restaurant, not a convenience store.

MATTHEW: Now you are generalizing.

HONG: Joking.

MATTHEW: Funny.

HONG: Yes, all Chinese families can use bamboo in the house. We all need good fortune.

MAI: **What are you saying?**
你在說什麼呀?

MATTHEW: It's okay…I'm sorry if I offended you with my gift.

HONG: I am not offended. But you should not be upset with me for "generalizing" your family if you are that way yourself.

MATTHEW: Okay, lilacs next time…if there is a next time.

HONG: I prefer sunflower.

MATTHEW: Sure.

Beat.

MAI: Kevin talk to you about us?

MATTHEW: Of course he did.

MAI: What he say?

MATTHEW: That you are closed-minded, controlling, and unaffectionate.

MAI: What?

MATTHEW: But he also said that you're generous, hard-working, protective and he wouldn't trade you for the world.

MAI: Unaffectionate? He did not think we love him?

MATTHEW: He knew that you loved him. He just never heard it. Sometimes hearing it helps.

HONG: Why you need to hear if you know?

MATTHEW: Because he's human and not a robot. Is saying "I love you" to your own son so hard?

HONG: It is not what we say, but what we do. We work hard to give him everything. That is our way.

MATTHEW: Your way might not have been enough, is all.

HONG: That is you. That does not mean it is us. We are not that kind of family.

MATTHEW: You were the kind that didn't communicate.

MAI: We talk to him.

HONG: Enough! You are not here to teach us how to be a better family.

MATTHEW: You're right, I'm not here to teach you anything. But you could have asked your son more questions. Kevin wanted to talk to you more.

HONG: Are you blaming us for what happen?

MATTHEW: I'm just saying things could have been different if you were more involved in his life. He tried to tell you that his bipolar was getting worse. You knew he was unstable.

MAI: Kevin bipolar is very hard for us to understand.

MATTHEW: You mean it was hard for you to accept?

MAI: We try…we think he just moody.

MATTHEW: There was nothing to think about. He was diagnosed by a doctor. He told you it was something that needed medication. But what, you thought it was just mood swings? It was a disease.

MAI: He was emotional about everything.

HONG: We do not believe happy sometime, then sad sometime so wrong.

MATTHEW: Well it was. He was often depressed. You both could have pressured him to open up to you more…

MAI: *(To HONG.)* How come we not know?

MATTHEW: How did he seem when he visited?

MAI: Fine.

MATTHEW: Happy?

MAI: Yes.

MATTHEW: Glad to be home?

MAI: I think so.

MATTHEW: Healthy?

HONG: What are you doing?

MATTHEW: She said you didn't know, so I'm just wondering how you could have missed all the hints.

MAI: Maybe we not ask enough questions.

HONG: He have mouth, too. If he want to talk more, he can talk more.

MATTHEW: How often did you call him?

MAI: I call him every week.

MATTHEW: I meant you, Mr. Lee.

HONG: Enough. I know my son.

MATTHEW: Then why are you trying to learn more about him through some stranger?

MAI: You close to Kevin—

HONG: **Enough! I don't want to hear anymore!**
够了, 我不要再聽下去!

MAI: **Relax, Hong. He is just trying to explain some things to us.**
別這樣了, 阿鴻, 他只是想跟我們解釋一些事情.

HONG: I talk to him like my parents talk to me. *(Beat.)* I ask him how he is. How is school? He always say, "fine." Everything is always "fine." Why I think something is wrong?

MATTHEW: It can't be "fine," when everything is always "fine."

MATTHEW and MAI attempt to interject during HONG's following speech.

HONG: Again, you think you know what is right. Just because I do not tell my son I love him, or hug him, or ask him a lot of question, does not mean I do not know how to be a father. I teach him how to be in society. To have manners, to be polite. To respect his elder. I raise him to understand what hard work mean, that money has to be earn. There is a lot more to being a father than saying "I love you." You do not have a child and maybe never will. You have no right to tell me what to do!

MATTHEW: Okay…I hear you, and I understand. All I'm saying is…Kevin didn't feel that you ever really talked to him, or cared to know who he really was. You never truly liked the fact that he was an artist, did you?

MAI: We did not mind.

MATTHEW: But you were never really happy about that, right?

Flashback to when KEVIN was a teenager.

HONG: **A painter? How will you make money?**
做畫家? 你能賺多少錢呀?

MAI: **Let him be.**

由得他吧.

HONG: **Kevin, think this through. Painting? How would you pay for rent and food? You have to eat, you know!**

凱文, 你想清楚. 畫畫? 要不要交房租, 要不要買菜? 你要不要吃飯!

MAI: **Son, we are just worried about your future.**

兒子呀, 我們是擔心你呀.

HONG: **You don't know how hard the real world is. You think not being afraid is enough? Huh? How will you raise a family?** *(Beat.)* **Well, it is something you need to think about!**

你知不知道這世界艱難, 你以為膽子夠就行, 你怎麼養家活口? 你要好好想想呀.

MAI: **It's very risky. Your dad would not have been able to give you the life you have if he continued to only paint.**

你這太冒險了. 如果你爸也只靠畫畫, 你以為他有辦法一手把你養大.

HONG: **No, I couldn't just do what I wanted to. I had responsibilities. I had you!**

不可能. 我不能想做什麼就做什麼. 我有責任. 我有你!

MAI: **He's not blaming you for anything. Your father is simply saying—**

他不是什麼都怪你, 你爸爸是說一

HONG: **I don't want to argue with you anymore!** *(Beat.)* **That's right, when things don't sound good to you, you run up to your room and hide.**

我不跟你吵了. 好吧, 一講你不愛聽的, 你就躲到房間裡.

Beat.

MAI: **He is talented and stubborn.**
他有天份, 也很牛脾氣.

HONG: **You really think he is talented?**
你真的認為他有天份?

MAI: **You've seen his drawings since he was a kid, what do you think?**
你也看過他從小畫的畫, 你怎麼說?

HONG: **I think talent is not enough.**
光有天份是不夠的.

MAI: **You don't need to be your father, you know?**
你不需要跟你爸一樣.

HONG: **I'm not.**
我沒有.

MAI: **Then maybe we should let him be.**
那或許我們應該跟他說.

HONG: **I just don't want him to…do I have a choice?**
我只是真的不希望他…我有得選擇嗎?

Present.

MAI: But we never stop him after that.

MATTHEW: You never encouraged him, either. Kevin wasn't making hundreds of thousands of dollars, but he was making it work. Yeah, he also worked at a Second Cup. At least it wasn't Starbucks, and every artist has a day job.

HONG: Why you say all this? We could do this, we could do that.

MATTHEW: He could have used more support.

HONG: Something wrong with you! I lose my son. And now you want me to say sorry for everything? That what you want?

MATTHEW: No…I want you to understand…Kevin would want you to—

HONG: No! You want. You don't know—you have no way to know for sure what Kevin want.

MATTHEW: I know he would've wanted me to be at his funeral. I know he wanted us all to get together. I know he wanted you to understand—

HONG: I understand! I know what I want to do for him. I give him the best funeral I can afford. The best cemetery, not too crowded. The best tombstone. The best…everything. I want the best for him. When he alive, and now! All you have are ideas. You think I should listen to my son more, talk to him more, understand his feelings. I set up good life for him. I make sure his path is good. All he has to do is walk on it!

HONG is clenching his heart as though he might fall over. He sits down, possibly away from the dinner table in the living room area.

MATTHEW: Are you okay? I'm sorry, I didn't mean to…

HONG: What you mean not matter. What you do matter.

MATTHEW: I'll get you some water.

HONG: No, I don't need you to—

MAI: **Stop it!** (夠 了.) It's okay, Matt. Let me.

MAI brings HONG a glass of water.

Calm down, don't get so frustrated. Here, drink this. (冷靜點, 幹什麼氣成這樣. 來, 喝點水.)

HONG drinks some of the water. Beat.

MATTHEW: I'm sorry for upsetting you.

MAI: Mr. Lee also very passionate. Kevin get his temper from his father. *(To HONG.)* **Do you want more water?** (你還要水嗎?)

HONG: **I have enough.**

夠了.

MAI: Matt, we help him go to Vancouver. We give money for him to go. We support him the way we know how.

HONG: **You don't have to explain things to him.**

你不用跟他解釋.

MATTHEW: He would have loved for you to show up to one of his art openings.

MAI: Too far away.

MATTHEW: Maybe you could have taken some time off and gone there?

MAI: Not easy to take time off, Matt. We always have to be around to look after restaurant.

MATTHEW: He thought you weren't all that interested, so he didn't push you. But he really wanted you to come.

MAI: He always say he was—

MATTHEW: Fine?

MAI: Yes.

MATTHEW: The way he looked at the world around him was…special. He'd make me stop and observe things I'd usually just walk by. He was able to see colours in the mundane I would never notice, and brought them out in his work. Kevin wanted you to know how good he was. There was this abstract piece of Toronto and Vancouver he did a few months after we met. His heart really was in both cities. It was the first time I realized how talented he was. Kevin's love for his work was contagious…he inspired me to do more of what I loved.

Beat.

MAI: What?

HONG: **Why are you still talking to him? Tell him to go.**

你還在跟他談什麼, 叫他走吧.

MAI: **Don't be like that.** (別這樣.) What, Matt? What did Kevin make you do?

Beat.

MATTHEW: Sing. I loved singing when I was a kid. You know, did the whole choir thing and took music throughout high school. But to pursue it any further wasn't realistic. I just kept telling myself there is a huge commonality between music and math. What I love about both is the specificity. With math, it's about being exact, precise, calculated. With music, you need to be just as precise, but with rhythm, beat, and keys.

MAI: Wah.

HONG: *(Sarcastically.)* Good for you.

MAI: Kevin painting make you want to sing?

MATTHEW: He reminded me of how it felt to be on stage.

MAI: You on stage before?

MATTHEW: Actually, last year Kevin pushed me to compete in an *American Idol*-like competition.

MAI: *American Idol,* Hong. You love to watch *American Idol.*

HONG: Hm.

MATTHEW: Well, it wasn't THE *American Idol.* It was a competition in our neighbourhood called "West End Idol."

HONG: "West End Idol," Mai. Not same thing.

MAI: **It doesn't matter, he sang in a competition.**
有什麼關係, 他是參加歌唱比賽.

HONG: **So what? Big deal.**
那又怎樣, 了不起啊?

MAI: You win?

MATTHEW: Not exactly.

HONG: See?

MATTHEW: I placed second. It was for fun, anyways.

MAI: Oh, wah, second place. You must be very good.

MATTHEW: I'm not bad.

MAI: Sing something for us.

MATTHEW: Uh…no, really, I can't.

MAI: Please.

MATTHEW: Not now.

MAI: Hong, you want to hear Matt sing?

Beat.

HONG: I love to. Please, go ahead.

Beat.

MATTHEW: Well…okay. Um…

Flashback to "West End Idol."

MATTHEW: *(To Kevin.)* This is for you, babe.

MATTHEW starts to sing "Over The Rainbow." He sings it beautifully flowing into…

Flashback to MAI and HONG at home when KEVIN was a baby. MAI is holding KEVIN, and HONG is by her. MAI is putting KEVIN to sleep humming the same song MATTHEW is singing ("Over The Rainbow") and slowly beginning to sing it herself. After a while, she sets KEVIN down into his crib.

HONG: **What are you singing?**

你在唱什麼?

MAI: **"Over the Rainbow."**

飛越彩虹.

HONG: **Where did you learn that song?**

那裡學來的?

MAI: **They taught it to us in night school. Singing a song is teaching me English.**

英文夜校. 唱歌學英文.

HONG: **Sing Chinese to him**, Mai. Y**ou don't want him to not know his mother tongue.**

唱中文歌給他聽, 別讓他以後連自己的母語都不會聽.

MAI: **I know, I know, relax, it's just one song.**

我知道, 別緊張, 一首歌, 沒那麼嚴重.

HONG: **Listen to me sing.**
聽我來唱.

HONG starts to sing a Chinese ballad. MAI continues to sing, "Over The Rainbow" to toy with him. Both melodies blend together, flowing into MATTHEW's singing in the "present." Transition to…

Present. MATTHEW finishes singing. Awkward silence.

MATTHEW: It was that bad?

MAI: No, no. Very good. You have beautiful voice.

HONG: Not bad.

MATTHEW: It was one of Kevin's favourite songs.

MAI: We know.

Beat.

MATTHEW: Anyways, I played it safe…but not Kevin. He pursued his passions wholeheartedly. He was always shamelessly himself, didn't care what people thought of him. I just wish he could have been more of who he was around both of you when he visited. I mean…be out…openly gay at home, here.

MAI: If he say something before…maybe I understand.

MATTHEW: He didn't think you would.

Flashback to MATTHEW talking to KEVIN in their apartment.

MATTHEW: What are you so afraid of? You don't even live with them anymore, it's not like they can kick you out. Christmas is as good as any other time to come out. It'll be like…an extra Christmas gift. Will you put that paintbrush down for a sec and listen to me?

I love you. I want you to be happy. And no matter how happy you are in Vancouver living your life with me, our friends, and pursuing your art…I think that something is still missing in you. When you go to that…dark place, it scares me because I can't do anything.

I think telling your parents will help. I know, I know…you come from a traditional Chinese family, but they've got to deal with it. Being gay is almost trendy nowadays. So please just do it this time when you get home…for me… for us…

You don't want to disappoint them…right. *(Beat.)*

Present.

MAI: We did not know for sure…but sometimes, before…I think maybe he was…

HONG: **Mai, what are you saying?**
阿美, 你在說什麼?

MAI: I sometimes feel he like boys. **Don't say you didn't know.** (不要說你不知道.) He have no girlfriend in high school. Not play hockey, not play baseball, not play—

MATTHEW: Whether someone plays a sport or not doesn't tell you if they're gay. I'm on a curling league.

MAI: Matt, you not help.

MATTHEW: Dodgeball? *(Beat.)* Never mind.

MAI: I am his mother. Deep down, I know. *(To HONG.)* You know too.

MATTHEW: What were you so afraid of?

MAI: That he will be hurt. That the world see him as not normal.

MATTHEW: That didn't happen. He had a lot of friends.

MAI: Yes, I think he maybe…queer, but not for sure.

MATTHEW: Why do you say "queer"?

MAI: Pride Festival, I see "queer" everywhere.

MATTHEW: Gay…gay! He was gay.

HONG: "Queer" sound less gay.

Awkward beat.

MAI: Tell me…when you first meet Kevin?

MATTHEW: It was a little over three years ago.

MAI: He just finish school.

MATTHEW: That's right.

MAI: We think he will come back home after he graduate. But no, he say he want to stay in Vancouver.

MATTHEW: It's a beautiful city.

MAI: So where you meet?

Flashback to gay dance club. Club music fades in. MATTHEW is at the club with KEVIN.

MATTHEW: Hi. "Kevin," you said? I'm Matthew, or Matt, whatever. *(Beat.)* Well, you said Kevin, or Kev whatever, so I thought I'd—never mind. *(Beat.)*

Yeah, I'm here with friends or at least I was. You? *(Beat.)* Oh come on, the fact that they're all coupled up is...cute. *(Beat.)* Cute like me? Haha, yeah...anyways...I like your piercing, the hole's a bit higher than the norm, it's... unique. *(Beat.)* Wait...where are you taking me? *(Beat.)* Nah, my friends might come back, let's just stay here. *(Beat.)* No, that's not true. I am into Asians. I mean it's not my preference but you're ...

Present for MAI and HONG. MATTHEW remains in the flashback at the dance club.

HONG: You are racist.

MAI: HONG!

HONG: He just say he not like Asian. What is wrong with Asian? Hm?

MAI: Let him explain.

MATTHEW: ...different. I'm sorry that came out wrong. I like all sorts of guys, just not typically Asian ones.

MAI: Just like how you only like Asian ladies when you young, Hong.

HONG: We meet in Vietnam, not much choice.

MATTHEW: The point is...you got my attention, I didn't expect it.

HONG: Why?

MATTHEW: Well...you're not typically Asian.

MAI: Typical?

MATTHEW: Yeah, come on, you know Asian men in the gay community have certain...connotations...

MAI: Connotations?

MATTHEW: Things we think Asians are like.

MAI: What kind of thing?

MATTHEW: Well…um…honestly? Okay…Asian men are thought to be effeminate, not very athletic, submissive, all bottoms—I mean, God, you're really putting me on the spot here…

HONG: That is stupid.

MATTHEW: I know, you're right, I admit it, I'm a bit prejudiced. Anyways, prove me wrong.

Transition to a few moments later at the dance club.

A Long Island for me. Thanks. Budweiser… interesting choice. I didn't see you as a beer drinker. *(MATTHEW has a sip of his drink.)* Yummy. Hey, there's nothing wrong with saying yummy. Tasty…better?

MATTHEW now also shifts back into the present.

From that night on we were inseparable. We ended up going to Denny's after the club. Boy, your son could eat! He had a sampler, a milkshake, and a piece of apple pie, at two in the morning. I just went for my usual Grand Slam, love my pancakes!

HONG: He still always look so skinny when he come home. He never eat enough.

MATTHEW: Oh, trust me, he ate…a lot. And he looked good. Like…reeeally good. I just wanted to… *(Beat.)*

MAI: How you remember all this?

MATTHEW: It was our first meal together. I guess you remember things like that with someone you love.

MAI: So what happen after you eat? At Denny's…?

MATTHEW: Well…um…I think we went our separate ways that night after we ate. Yeah…or probably we went back to my place…and…um…we took a Grand Slam to go.

MAI: You can do take-out at Denny's in Vancouver?

MATTHEW: Yes, yes you can…and Kevin licked the second Grand Slam clean. It was incredible. *(Beat.)* Chemistry is a weird thing. It's like this invisible string that ties you to someone, and you just want to be around each other all the time.

Flashback to MATTHEW with KEVIN at an apartment viewing.

MATTHEW: Sorry I'm late! Oh wow…big windows. *(Beat.)* An art studio, really? I think that room's better off as my office. Hardwood floors, nice, nice. Wow, the bedroom's huge. Yes, and of course even better, the closet's huge. Something you still need to get out of. *(Beat.)* Okay, okay, not now. *(Beat.)* All right, the big closet's yours, I'm not the one who's hiding. *(Beat.)* All right, I'm sorry, I'll stop. Stainless steel appliances are great, but it's not like you cook. *(Beat.)* Eight hundred dollars each…let me think about it…I'm kidding. *(Beat.)* I mean this place is pretty amazing. I don't need to commute all the way from Commercial Drive anymore. English Bay is at our doorstep. I'm game. *(Beat.)* Whoa, calm down. What's this? *(MATTHEW has a jade pendant on a necklace in his hands.)* Oh wow… yeah, I know it's jade. "Beauty, grace and purity?" Everything I am! I'm kidding! *(Beat.)* I love it, babe. Thank you.

Present.

MAI: We believe jade is invaluable.

HONG: You live together? Two men…

MATTHEW: We did.

HONG: You do not care what people think?

MATTHEW: No, I didn't…and you shouldn't, either.

HONG: Do not tell me that until you bring up a family with nothing but your bare hands. When I first come to this country, before I open restaurant, I work in a window factory.

MAI: **Don't talk about that now.**

現在提這幹嘛.

HONG: One break time, there was a water station. All the workers line up to fill cups with water. They keep pushing me back.

MAI: **That was a long time ago, Hong, why are you bringing it up?**

阿鴻, 古老十八代的東西提來幹嘛?

HONG: So I push one back. Then they gang up on me, start fight. They big group. I am one person. Boss not believe what I say. Back then, I do not know English. Boss look at me, think I start trouble, so he fire me. So…how you look, "What people think," does matter.

MAI: **Enough, enough.**

夠了, 夠啦.

Beat.

MATTHEW: I see…but we didn't get together to piss off the world…or you. We met and fell in love, we didn't know any other way. Kevin never cared what people thought. He only cared about what you thought. *(Beat.)* If that wasn't the case you might have gotten this sooner.

MATTHEW moves to the wrapped canvas that is set in the living room area, and picks it up.

This is what Kevin was going to give you.

MATTHEW hands MAI the wrapped canvas.

I found it in the closet. It was labeled, "To Mom and Dad." That's when I called you. I thought you should have it. *(Beat.)* Go on, open it.

MAI begins unwrapping the canvas. The canvas is unwrapped. Silence. MAI takes some time to turn the painting right-side up. It is of Kevin's attempt to write the Chinese character, "FAMILY," with the backdrop being a painting of Toronto and Vancouver melded together (perhaps featuring well-known landmarks from each city flowing into each other). MAI turns the canvas around to show HONG.

MAI: **Look, Hong.**

阿鴻, 你看.

HONG: **"Family."**

家.

MATTHEW: What does it say?

MAI: Family.

MATTHEW: Family. *(MATTHEW chuckles.)* Of course…and that's the painting I told you about. Toronto and Vancouver in one. They were both his home.

MAI: It is beautiful. Sometimes I think he forget about us.

MATTHEW: He never did.

HONG has approached the canvas by now.

HONG: It's very good. Very good. He remember where he come from.

MATTHEW: Yeah, he did. Who knows, maybe your ways can get him to the same place.

MAI: What place is that?

MATTHEW: His true self.

MAI: Thank you for bringing this to us, Matt.

MATTHEW: You're welcome. *(Beat.)* I was hoping you could share something with me.

MAI: What you mean?

MATTHEW: I'm planning to have a memorial for Kevin when I get back to Vancouver.

HONG: A memorial?

MATTHEW: We didn't really get a chance to say goodbye. It's an opportunity for everyone to say their farewells…have a bit of closure.

MAI: Oh.

MATTHEW: Nothing big, at a local art studio. Just a bunch of his friends. Everyone would love to hear a bit about Kevin from his parents. I was hoping you could write a few words for me to share.

Beat.

MAI: Yes.

HONG: No.

MATTHEW: Why not?

HONG: I do not have time to write anything.

MAI: **Don't be like that—**
別這樣一

MATTHEW: It's a celebration of your son's life, with his friends.

HONG: We do not know them. They do not know us.

MAI: What do you want me to write?

HONG: I say no.

MATTHEW: Anything…anything about Kevin at all. Doesn't have to be long, a few sentences will do.

HONG: The people that go…they all…

MATTHEW: Gay?

HONG: Yes.

MATTHEW: Some.

HONG: **Mai, we don't know the kinds of people that will be at this event.**
阿美. 我們都不認識那些人.

MAI: **It doesn't matter.**
沒關係.

MATTHEW: You don't have to worry Mr. Lee, we won't be there celebrating his sexuality. He did enough of that when he was alive, trust me.

HONG: If we are part of memorial, it will look like we are okay with Kevin being gay.

MATTHEW: Is that a bad thing? It'll be about time.

MAI: I will give you something tomorrow…

MATTHEW: Thank you, Mai.

HONG: I want no part of this.

MATTHEW: It's for Kevin.

HONG: It is for you. You want my son to be someone not normal.

MATTHEW: That's not true.

HONG: You want to make sure everyone know who he is in your eyes.

MATTHEW: You're totally twisting things around.

HONG: You make him into something he is not in front of all the people!

MATTHEW: I want to make him out to be who he was for everyone. I want people to know how special he was to me. Is that so wrong? I want people to know that he used to have this "goofy" smile, which was this cute, slanted grin he had when he was excited about something.

MAI: You really love him.

MATTHEW: Yeah.

HONG: Two men should not be together like that. *(To MAI.)* **That song make him gay.** (都是你那首歌惹的禍.)

MAI: **What are you talking about?**

你在講什麼?

HONG: **That rainbow song, that gay song you sing all the time is what made him gay.**

那首彩虹歌. 天天唱, 不是同志都給你唱成同志.

MAI: Don't listen to him.

MATTHEW: I don't know what he's saying.

MAI: **How can you say that I made our son gay?**
你怎麼可以說是我把他變成同志的?

MATTHEW: What are you saying? What's happening?

MAI: He say I sing, "Over The Rainbow," make Kevin queer.

MATTHEW: *(Processing what he just heard.)* He said you singing, "Over The Rainbow" to Kevin made him queer…what?

HONG: You lead him down wrong path too.

MAI whacks HONG.

MATTHEW: What path do you think I led your son down?

HONG: If not for you, he will still be here. He will still be normal.

MATTHEW: Normal, gee…I wonder what you mean by that?

HONG: You know what I mean.

MATTHEW: Yes, I made your son gay. I admit it. It's all because of me.

HONG: He not like that before you.

MATTHEW: You mean he wasn't gay.

HONG: Yes, call it what you want.

MATTHEW: You sure he didn't "like boys" before he met me?

HONG: Why else he become that way? He not like that before Vancouver. If I know for sure he was learning bad ways…

MATTHEW: Bad ways?

HONG: I would have…

MATTHEW: You would have what? Tried to change him?

HONG: I would have help him…there are doctors…

MATTHEW: Your son didn't need to be fixed!

HONG: If you could like girls, would you? If you can choose?

MATTHEW: We can't choose.

HONG: But…if you can?

Beat.

MATTHEW: I don't know…maybe. Life might be easier.

HONG: So, can you blame me to want to give my son an easier life?

MATTHEW: No…but you can't make a gay man straight.

HONG: You make my son gay.

MATTHEW: How?

HONG: How I know? I not gay.

MATTHEW: This is ridiculous. I can't—wow.

MAI: Mr. Lee need time.

MATTHEW: I'm sorry…I need a smoke.

MATTHEW heads to the door.

HONG: Go!

MAI: You smoke? Kevin smoke too?

MATTHEW: He was an artist, of course he smoked. He thought it made him look hip.

MAI: Hip?

MATTHEW: Cool. It just rained again…maybe I'll get more gay by catching a rainbow.

HONG: Smoking give you cancer!

MATTHEW has exited out the porch door. Beat.

HONG: **Good job on the Kung Pao chicken tonight.** *(Beat.)* **Very good. Everything is very good.** *(Beat.)* **I'll take care of cleaning up when he leaves. You just rest.**

今晚的宮保雞丁很好. 樣樣都很好. 他走了, 我來洗碗, 你早點休息.

MAI cleans up, giving HONG the silent treatment.

HONG: **Hey, stop…stop while you're ahead. I'm your husband. Why are you being like this to me over that kid? Mai, I'm talking to you.**

你見好就收啦. 我是你丈夫. 為了那孩子, 你幹嘛跟我這樣? 我在跟你說話.

MAI: **You promised me that you would keep it together tonight.**

你答應我今天晚上好自為之的.

HONG: **I don't want to know him. You think he will bring us closer to Kevin, not me.**

我不想認識他, 是你認為他可以幫我們和凱文接近. 我可沒說.

MAI: **Then why did you agree to have him come?**

那你幹什麼答應讓他來?

HONG: **Because he had something of our son's.**

因為他說他有我兒子的東西.

MAI: **He could have mailed it. But you finally agreed to have him visit.**

他可以用寄的. 可你還是答應讓他來.

HONG: **Because you wanted it...because he kept calling and wouldn't give up. Because I wanted to see if he was to blame for what happened.**

以為你要呀. 因為他天天打電話來呀, 因為我要看看到底是不是該怪他.

MAI: **You already decided he is to blame because he is gay. Give him a chance. I want to know my son, Hong, everything about him. Don't ruin it.**

你早就因為他是同志， 而認為該怪他. 你就給他一次機會嘛. 我要知道我兒子的一切. 你不要把事情搞砸.

HONG: **What else is there to know?**

還要知道些什麼?

MAI: **We've talked about this! That last time we talked to Kevin on the phone...**

我們講過呀. 凱文最後打電話來的那次…

Flashback. Phone rings, and MAI picks up. It's KEVIN on the other line.

MAI: **Are you okay? Work is good?** *(Beat.)* **Are you not well? You're with Matthew again? No?** *(Beat.)* **Here, you should talk to him. Just a moment...Hong!**

好嗎? 工作順利嗎? 不舒服? 你跟馬修在一起? 沒有? 你來跟他講…等一會.阿鴻!

HONG gets on the phone.

HONG: **Hello. How are things?** *(Beat.)* **Do you want me to send you some money? You eating enough?** *(Beat.)* **Here, talk to your mom.**

喂…怎麼樣? 要不要寄錢給你? 吃飽了嗎? 來, 你媽跟你說.

MAI takes the phone.

MAI: *(To HONG.)* **You finished talking so quickly.** *(Into phone.)* **If you ever need to talk to us about something, just say it.** (*Beat.)* **Okay, take care of yourself. Okay?** *(Beat.)* **Okay, I—***(Kevin's hung up. To HONG.)* **He said he loves me.**

這麼快. 你有什麼想講的你就說吧. 自己照顧自己. 好. 我…他說他很愛你.

Present.

HONG: **So what?**

那又怎樣?

MAI: **Matt wasn't there with him. He was always there.**

馬修沒跟他在一起, 平時都有.

HONG: **So what if he wasn't there?**

那又怎樣?

MAI: **Kevin was my son. I know when something is wrong. I heard it in his voice…and he said he loved me.**

凱文是我兒子, 我知道不對路, 我聽得出來. 而且他會說他愛我.

HONG: **Maybe he finally missed us and wanted to come home. You're reading too much into it.**

也許他終於想家想回來. 你想太多了.

MAI: **No, Hong. I want to talk to Matt some more. I need to know exactly what happened that night.**

不, 我要再跟馬修談談, 我要知道那天晚上到底發生什麼事.

HONG: **Why don't we just ask him, if that's what you want? I'll go out there right now and ask him.**

既然這樣那就直接了當跟他說嘛. 我現在就出去問他.

MAI: **What are you going to ask him? "Excuse me, did you do something that night that caused Kevin to drown?" Do you think he will admit it if he was at all responsible?** (*Beat.*) **I can see he loved Kevin, so I don't get it. We just have to keep listening to everything.**

你要問他什麼? "對不起, 你跟凱文講了什麼害他淹死的?" 你想他會承認什麼嗎? 我看得出來他愛凱文, 所以我才弄不懂? 我們就繼續聽下去吧?

HONG: **He thinks he knows our son better than we do. How can I listen to that garbage and not say anything back?**

他就是認為他比我們更了解我兒子. 胡說八道, 你叫我不跟他罵回去才怪!

MAI: **For me, Hong. Please, go out there and talk to him. Tell him you want him to stay.**

就算為了我吧. 阿鴻. 你就出去跟他說你要他留下來.

HONG: **I…really can't—**

我, 我辦不到—

MAI: **Please, do this one thing for me will you? All I'm asking is for one night you do what I ask.**

我就求你這一次吧. 就一個晚上你聽我的. 行嗎?

HONG: **But—**
可是—

MAI: **Don't you want to know the truth?**
難道你不想知道真相?

Beat. HONG heads out to the porch. MAI continues to clean up the dishes.

Outside on the porch, HONG approaches MATTHEW. Beat.

HONG: You not smoking.

MATTHEW: Forgot my light.

Beat. HONG hands MATTHEW a light from his pant pocket.

MATTHEW: Thanks. *(Beat.)* I also left my cigarettes in my jacket pocket inside.

Long beat. HONG takes out a pack of cigarettes, opens it and offers it to MATTHEW. MATTHEW accepts the offer and takes a cigarette from the pack. MATTHEW lights his cigarette and hands the light back. He smokes. Beat. HONG looks at the pack of cigarettes for a moment. He takes a cigarette out, lights it and smokes.

MATTHEW: Cancer?

Beat.

HONG: My son look hip like me?

MATTHEW: Your friends were right, you are funny.

HONG: Mai not know I smoke again, but I need something. Smoking…help me.

MATTHEW: Helps you how?

Beat.

HONG: It help me remember…

MATTHEW: Kevin? *(Beat.)* He wanted to live the dream you had for him. Become a businessman, dentist, doctor…straight. He wanted that so badly. But it just wasn't who he was.

HONG: Enough…what happen that night?

MATTHEW: What night?

HONG: The night Kevin died.

MATTHEW: What do you mean?

HONG: Mai think you…nothing. We do not have to talk.

MATTHEW: Mai thinks what?

HONG: She think you…know everything. You can get us closer to Kevin.

MATTHEW: I can try.

HONG: No more talk. We can just stand here…go back in few minute.

MATTHEW: Aren't you tired of it?

HONG: What?

MATTHEW: Pretending. When Kevin was alive you were pretending everything was fine. Him being bipolar, your relationship with him, his sexuality. And now…with me, you're just trying to fake it to make Mai happy. Why can't you just talk to me?

HONG: We have nothing to talk about! You are here because Mai think you have all the answers. Not me. I let you stay for Mai, that is it.

MATTHEW: Oh, I thought you had me here so you can have someone to blame. So you won't feel guilty for what happened.

HONG: Why I need to feel guilty? I did nothing wrong.

MATTHEW: You don't know your own son!

HONG raises his hand about to strike MATTHEW. He holds back…

HONG: He died because of you!

MATTHEW: How?

HONG: If you never met Kevin…everything will be different.

MATTHEW: You're right, things would be. He might've met someone else…some other man for you to blame. I am more than just some guy Kevin met at a dance club one night, Mr. Lee. Stop looking at me as though I'm the monster that wrecked your son's life.

HONG: You did!

MATTHEW: He grew up, he changed, he grew into who he was meant to be. You need to stop blaming me, or anyone else for what happened.

HONG: You keep him in Vancouver. We tell him to come home, but you keep him there.

MATTHEW: He chose to live there. I didn't force him to stay. And how was him staying in Vancouver a reason for what happened?

HONG: Because we cannot protect him!

MATTHEW: He didn't need your protection.

HONG: He drown!

Beat.

MATTHEW: Really? You truly believe everything that led to Kevin dying was because he turned out gay, because of me?

HONG: I know you not help!

MATTHEW: I'm outta here.

HONG: Good!

MATTHEW puts out his cigarette and enters the house.

Inside, MATTHEW sees MAI with a large platter of mango pudding.

MATTHEW: I have to go—

MAI: No, no, sit. We have dessert. Mango pudding. Why Mr. Lee not come in?

MATTHEW: He's just finishing…uh…getting some fresh air.

MAI: Matt.

MATTHEW: Yes?

MAI: I know he smoke.

MATTHEW: Oh, sorry, I didn't mean to—why don't you just tell him you know?

MAI: He try to hide it from me. So I let him hide it. He feel better.

MATTHEW: But what if he doesn't really want to hide it from you? Maybe he's just afraid you'll be upset.

MAI: Then I hope he will tell me. Up to him. *(Beat.)* Sit down, we have dessert!

MATTHEW: I'm sorry, I can't, I really gotta run.

MAI: Why, what happen? You do not like mango pudding?

MATTHEW: No, I love it. But you know this isn't working. Mr. Lee doesn't want me here. He's not listening to anything I have to say, it's pointless. I'm sorry I can't help you clean up.

MAI: We not finish. Mr. Lee need some time to open up. I go get him, you stay.

MATTHEW: He's not going to listen.

MAI: I make sure he listen.

MATTHEW: You can't—

HONG enters.

MAI: Matt, sit down! *(To HONG.)* **What did you say to him? He wants to leave now.** (你跟他說了什麼? 他這就要走.)

HONG: **Good.**
很好.

MAI: **I'm not done hearing about my son.**
我還有很多事情要知道.

MATTHEW: Excuse me…

MAI: Matt, wait.

HONG: **Let him go.**
讓他走.

MAI: **I want to know more.**
我還要知道.

HONG: **We don't need his stories, Mai.**
我們不需要聽他講故事.

MAI: **My son is already dead. Please!**
我兒子已經死了. 我求求你!

HONG: **He's my son too!**
他也是我的兒子.

MATTHEW: Please stop arguing.

MAI: We not arguing. We just talking. Right, Hong?

HONG: We talking.

MATTHEW: It sounded…never mind. It really was good to meet you, Mai.

MAI: Kevin love mango pudding.

MATTHEW: I know. He introduced me to it.

MAI: Eat some before you go.

MATTHEW: I can't.

MAI: Matt, why you like this?

MATTHEW: I'm not like anything. This was a mistake.

MAI: Not mistake. Sit down.

HONG: **Let him go.**
讓他走.

MATTHEW: Good night, Mai. Good night, Mr. Lee.

MAI walks to block the door. She still has the mango pudding in her hands.

MAI: Sit.

MATTHEW: Mai, please.

HONG: **He should have left already.**
他早該走了.

MAI: **Be quiet.** (閉嘴.) Matt, stop.

MATTHEW: Let's not make this any harder. Please move out of the way.

HONG: **You're being crazy, Mai.**
你瘋了. 阿美.

MAI: **Then let me be crazy. I don't care.**
我就發瘋給你看. 我不管了.

MATTHEW walks towards the door.

MAI: Ahhhhhh!

MAI intentionally smashes the platter of mango pudding on the ground. Beat.

HONG: **Mai.**
阿美.

MATTHEW: You okay? Let me help you—

HONG: You help enough. Look what happen now. **Mai, what are you doing?** (阿美, 你在幹什麼呀?)

MAI: Big mess I make.

MATTHEW: Big mess we all made.

MAI: I clean.

HONG: **What are you doing? Sit.**
你在幹什麼? 坐下吧.

HONG grabs a broom and dustpan to sweep up the mess. MAI goes to the fridge.

MAI: **Let me be.**
我來.

MATTHEW: Mai, why don't you sit down for a bit?

MAI takes out another platter of mango pudding from the fridge.

You have another one?

MAI: We run Chinese restaurant.

MATTHEW: Right.

MAI also brings bowls and spoons to the dinner table. She scoops mango pudding into the bowls. She sits and eats a spoonful of the mango pudding. HONG and MATTHEW simply watch MAI.

Beat.

MAI: Matt…please sit. **Hong, sit down and eat.** (阿鴻. 來坐. 吃.)

HONG puts down the broom.

MAI: Tea? *(Beat.)* Matt, tea? Please, sit. I make tea.

MATTHEW: No. I've been here for too long already.

HONG: He take away our son, Mai. He kill Kevin. **Are you blind?** (你是瞎了眼嗎?)

MATTHEW: There! You hear that Mai? He finally said it out in the open. That's what you wanted to say all along, isn't it?

HONG: Yes!

MAI: No, stop!

MATTHEW: That's not fair. I've had enough of this. I tried, Mai.

MAI: Mr. Lee need—

MATTHEW: No, no more time. No more talking. He's not listening, so what's the point?

MAI: I listen.

HONG: I listen too, but what you say…is garbage!

HONG and MAI's following lines are delivered on top of what MATTHEW is saying.

MATTHEW: Mr. Lee, I'm in your house, and I want to give you the respect you deserve, but you're not making it easy. Your son is dead! And he never got to have the family he wanted because he thought he wasn't good enough for you. Because you made him believe he wasn't normal.

(HONG: I not make him believe anything? He think what he want.)

MATTHEW: His bipolar was nothing to worry about. Him being gay is just a phase. It wasn't. He was a fucking fag.

(HONG: Get out! Get out now!)

(MAI: Stop! Both of you, stop!)

MATTHEW: I am too…and we were in love, and made love. If that's too much for you to handle, too bad. Don't try to find out who your son really was. I just feel sad for you.

HONG throws one of the small bowls of mango pudding towards MATTHEW. He misses.

HONG: Get out! You said you leaving, so go! How dare you talk to me like that? Who you think you are?

MATTHEW goes for his jacket, puts it on, then heads for his carry-on during the following.

That's it, Mai. Get him out! (把他打出去!) Get out!

MAI: **He's leaving. Now what?**
他要走, 現在呢?

HONG: **So what? Good!**
怎樣? 很好呀!

MAI: **You promised!**
你答應的.

HONG: **I did my best!**
我盡力了!

MAI: **Did you?**
你有嗎?

HONG: **Did I not?**
我沒有嗎?

MAI: **Aahhhhhhgg! You still don't understand!**
哎呀, 你怎麼總不明白!

HONG: **Mai, stop being crazy!**
阿美你不要再發神經!

MAI: **I need more—**
我需要知道更多一

HONG: **More what?**
更多什麼?

MAI: **Truth!**
真相!

MATTHEW has everything he needs and is about to exit through the porch door.

MAI: Matt…stop. Please stay!

HONG: **You need to let him—**
你就讓他一

MAI: Matt, stay.

MATTHEW: We don't need to do this anymore. You got what Kevin left for you. I met you. You met me. It's enough.

MAI: Where you go the night Kevin died?

MATTHEW stops in his tracks.

MATTHEW: Excuse me?

MAI: You not with him. Where you go?

MATTHEW: Um…uh, I was out, I guess.

MAI: Out?

MATTHEW: Yes.

MAI: Why you not with Kevin?

MATTHEW: We had our own lives, too.

MAI: But he not well that night, and you not there.

MATTHEW: I'm sorry, um…how do you know this?

MAI: He call me. He told me he was by himself that night.

MATTHEW: But you didn't even know who I was.

MAI: I not know who you are with Kevin, but I hear your name many times. Kevin always talk about going out with his "good friend" Matthew. He say you at the movies that night.

MATTHEW: Okay, yeah, I was at the movies. Why did you ask if you already knew?

MAI: I want you tell me…

MATTHEW: Tell you what?

MAI: Who you go with?

MATTHEW: When?

MAI: To see movie.

MATTHEW: A friend...why are you asking me all this?

MAI: I don't understand why you at movies! That night Kevin not feeling good. You say you love him. Why you not there?

MATTHEW: I was!

MAI: You were not!

Beat.

MATTHEW: A few days before...we got into a big fight.

MAI: What?

Flashback to MATTHEW and KEVIN in their apartment. MAI and HONG engage in dialogue but they remain in the present.

MATTHEW: Of course you feel sick, after all the partying you did last night.

MAI: Partying?

MATTHEW: Drugs! Tell me what letter of the alphabet you're onto right now, I have a hard time keeping track.

HONG: You say you know him!

MATTHEW: No, I don't know, that's why I'm asking. If you're going to throw up, do it in the washroom, I'm not cleaning up your mess.

MAI: And then what?

MATTHEW: You know what? Screw this…I'm done. I can't do this anymore. Did you hear me? I said I can't do this anymore.

MAI: What you mean?

MATTHEW: This…us…this way…I can't. You always say you'll tone it down, but when? After Doug's birthday party this weekend—Jesus! Are you listening to yourself? Really? The fact that you even had to ask.

MAI: He say he will try.

MATTHEW: I don't want you to tone things down, and I don't think you can. I want you…to be…you, whoever that is. I just think…maybe this is you growing up, and I'm not where you are right now. I can't be where you are right now…I'm sorry.

HONG: What you saying?

MATTHEW: I don't know what I'm saying—I mean, I do know. We should probably take some time off. Yeah, I need to clear my mind, think some stuff through.

MAI: You leave him?

MATTHEW: I didn't say I want to break up with you, stop!

MAI: Then what you saying?

MATTHEW: Why are you forcing me to say it? For once in your life can you just let things be, and stop trying to control everything? I did love that part of you, but it's getting out of hand. Okay, fine, no! I don't love your controlling, obsessive ways anymore!

MAI: You say you love him.

MATTHEW: All right, then I don't love you!

MAI: Say again.

MATTHEW: You want me to say it? Really? I'll say it. I think we should break up! I want to break up with you!

HONG: You end it.

MATTHEW: It's over! We're over! *(Beat.)* Happy now?

Everyone shifts back to present.

MAI: No.

MATTHEW: We weren't together anymore okay! *(Beat.)* I thought he would be okay. I didn't think…I'm sorry, maybe I should have told you sooner.

MAI: Yes.

MATTHEW: The break-up might have hit him harder than I thought it would…which might have caused him to go overboard with all the drugs. I don't know if it did, I just—

HONG: My son is gone because you leave him?

MATTHEW: I don't know. I wish I knew he was taking it that hard.

MAI: You the only one who can help him then.

MATTHEW: I couldn't—I did, for a really long time. But it was scary, and I couldn't bear seeing him go down that road anymore.

MAI: If you really love him, you push forward. You not give up.

MATTHEW: It felt like I had no choice. It was as though he pushed me out of love.

HONG: Love is not here only when it is easy for you.

MATTHEW: I've been through hard times with Kevin. But you don't know how much it hurts to love someone who doesn't seem to be there, even when they're standing right in front of you.

MAI: What you mean?

MATTHEW: His bipolar…he was moody, never satisfied, would flip out all the time over little things. When he was depressed, I'd look into his eyes but not see him.

HONG: If you know he is sad a lot, why you not check on him?

MATTHEW: Now you wish I was with your son all the time.

HONG: I wish you never meet him. But you already meet, so if you able to help…

MATTHEW: No one knew what was going to happen. Not me, not you, not Kevin. It could have easily been like any other night. He'd go out, and when he came back, I'd end up getting him Gatorade or whatever else he needed. I didn't know he was going to party again and go down to the beach by himself.

HONG: Not like any night…he died!

MATTHEW: I know that.

MAI: I told you something wrong that night, Hong.

HONG: It was late. What we do? Fly over there?

MATTHEW: You knew.

MAI: No, we not know he was going to…

MATTHEW: After the phone call, why didn't you call me to check in?

MAI: We not have your number.

MATTHEW: We could have done something…together…

MAI: If we know each other then…

HONG: We would say more…on the phone…

MATTHEW: You had twenty-five years to say more.

HONG: And you should be there for him, not go see movie! Why you not stay with him a few night longer?

MATTHEW: I wish I was there for him too!

Beat.

MAI: You want our forgiveness? That why you come?

MATTHEW: No…maybe—I don't know…I told you, I wanted to give one last thing to Kevin, to share what I knew about him…with you. It was the least I could do for him.

MAI: I wish we share earlier, we could maybe help him together. *(Beat.)* You really…love my son?

MATTHEW: Yes.

MAI: More than anything in the world? Will you give your life for him?

Beat.

MATTHEW: I don't know if I'd give my life for anyone.

Beat.

MAI: Maybe Hong is right.

MATTHEW: Mai—

MAI: Maybe we blame you, but not because you are gay. Not because you are in relationship with our son. But because you did not love him…enough. He did not have anyone else in Vancouver. He think he have you…but no.

MATTHEW: He did…for a while.

MAI: You choose bad time to end your love. Hong, if we only accept him…for everything…

MATTHEW: I'm sorry…I wish I could have changed things.

MAI: Me too.

MATTHEW: So…can you forgive me…for not being there… for—

MAI: —not loving my son enough?

MATTHEW: I guess.

Beat.

MAI: No, I cannot.

Beat.

MATTHEW: This isn't right.

HONG: My son die is not right.

MAI: Matthew. You should go.

MATTHEW: This is it, huh? *(Beat.)* What if I want to stay for a while longer?

MAI: No reason for that.

MATTHEW: I want to sit here for a bit.

MAI: Why?

MATTHEW: Just sit and remember Kevin.

MAI: Matthew. No.

Beat.

MATTHEW: I see. You got what you wanted…an explanation for the unexplainable—your son's death. Now that you can pin it on me, you have no use for me anymore.

MAI: Go now.

MATTHEW: You're all I have left to remember him by, too.

MAI: You choose to live by memory. You choose to leave our son when he needed you!

MATTHEW: I know that! Do you think I don't feel any guilt? But you can't just blame me, and move on. We're all at fault, including Kevin. He wasn't perfect. I wasn't perfect. We didn't have the perfect relationship. We tried to make it work, and it just didn't. That's what happened. If you were hoping for a sweet, fairytale-like story with no problems about your son, and us together, I don't have it. Our lives were not that story, and that's the truth.

MAI: Please…go.

Beat.

MATTHEW: I loved him as much as I knew how.

MATTHEW takes off the jade necklace and offers it to HONG. HONG accepts it.

Thanks for dinner.

MATTHEW exits. Beat.

MAI: **I need some time to myself. I think I want to stay at my sister's tonight.**

我需要一個人冷靜一下, 今天晚上我到我妹家.

HONG: **He's gone now…everything's okay.**
他走了… 沒事了.

MAI: **No, it's not. We lost our son, and only now we know everything.**
不是沒事了, 我失去我兒子, 可到現在才明白真相.

HONG: **So you're just going to walk away from me?**
你就這樣丟下我?

MAI: **I just need to think things through.**
我只是要把事情想清楚.

HONG: **What is there to think through? I'm your husband.**
還有什麼要想清楚? 我是你老公.

MAI: **I don't know, I just want to run away from everything.**
我不知道, 我只是想一個人躲起來.

HONG: **Like how Matthew ran away from Kevin? You want to be just like him?**
就像馬修需要離開凱文一樣? 你也想學他一樣?

MAI: **I'm not being—**
我沒有—

HONG: **If you leave me now you will be like him.**
你要現在離開我, 你就會跟他一樣.

MAI: **Just give me a few minutes.**
你等我一下.

MAI exits. HONG picks up the painting and embraces it.

Long beat.

HONG notices something stuck on the back of the frame. It is a folded up piece of paper. He unfolds it, and discovers it is a letter from KEVIN. HONG reads it.

Beat.

MAI enters.

MAI: **I can clean up, you—what is that?**
我來收一下…這是什麼?

HONG: **A letter from Kevin.**
兒子的信.

HONG hands MAI the letter. She reads it.

MAI: "Dear Mom and Dad…"

Flashback. The letter from KEVIN turns into a letter of acceptance from an art school in Vancouver.

MAI: **He got accepted.**
他申請到學校了.

HONG: **Got accepted to what?**
哪個學校?

MAI: **The art school in Vancouver.**
溫哥華的藝術學校.

HONG: **My father left him money to go to school wherever he wants. Now he's leaving us and going to Vancouver to study art. How is he going to make a living?**
我爸留給他的錢說讓他去自己想念的學校, 現在可好, 跑到溫哥華去搞藝術. 真不知道他以後怎麼生活?

Lights up on MATTHEW, in present day at the cemetery, intercut with the flashback scene with MAI and HONG.

MATTHEW: Hey, what's up? Been a while, huh?

MAI: **Hong, relax.**
阿鴻, 別擔心啦.

HONG: **He's changed, Mai.**
阿美, 他變了.

MATTHEW: So much has changed since you've been gone.

MAI: **He's growing up.**
他長大了.

HONG: **He's a different person.**
變了個人似的.

MATTHEW: I think your dad is changing into a different kinda person.

MAI: **He's still your son.**
他還是你兒子.

HONG: **He has an earring.**
他還戴耳環.

MATTHEW: He called this morning, and told me where I'd find you…

MAI: **It's a phase.**
過一陣就沒事的.

HONG: **And his behavior is so erratic lately.**
他最近的情緒很不穩定.

MATTHEW: …then he hung up. Well, baby steps I guess.

MAI: **That's what kids do nowadays.**
現在的小孩就這樣.

HONG: **They get piercings and piss off their parents?**
鑽個耳洞來氣我們?

MATTHEW: I really pissed him off last night.

MAI: **What are you so afraid of?**
你怕什麼?

HONG: **Nothing. I just...he's different.**
沒有, 只覺得他…變了個人似的.

MATTHEW: We had our differences...but they clearly love you.

MAI: **We went through this already—**
我們談過的—

HONG: **No, I mean different from everyone else.**
我的意思是他跟別人都不一樣.

MATTHEW: They're trying to show it now.

MAI: **What do you mean different?**
你說有什麼不一樣?

HONG: **He's not like other boys.**
他跟其他男孩子不一樣.

MATTHEW: I hope you can see it.

MAI: **You really don't see it, do you?**
你真看不出來?

MATTHEW: I hope you're goofy-smiling.

HONG: **See what?**

看出什麼?

Lights snap out.